MW00696372

An Apache Indian Community

Greg Moskal

Rosen
REAL
READERS

The Rosen Publishing Group, Inc.
New York

Published in 2001 by The Rosen Publishing Group, Inc.
29 East 21st Street, New York, NY 10010

Book Design: Ronald A. Churley

Photo Credits: Cover and all interior photos by J.J. Foxx.

ISBN: 0-8239-8156-8
6-pack ISBN: 0-8239-8558-X

Manufactured in the United States of America

Contents

Clay Geronimo

My name is Clay Geronimo. I live in Mescalero, New Mexico. I am nine years old, and I am proud to be Apache. I am also proud to be **related** to Geronimo, a famous Apache leader who lived more than 100 years ago. Geronimo was a great **medicine man**. We believe that medicine men and women have special powers over sickness and evil spirits. Geronimo was also a great leader who fought to keep the Apache people safe.

Clay rides a horse just like Geronimo did long ago.

Clay's Home and Animals

My family lives on Geronimo Loop on the Mescalero Apache **Reservation**. Our reservation is near the White Mountains. The mountains are **sacred** to our people.

This summer I went to 4-H Steer School. I took Alfred, my new steer. A steer is a young male ox. I learned about taking care of big animals. Taking care of Alfred is a lot of hard work! I like feeding Alfred, who lives on my grandpa's farm. I also like to ride my horse, Ernie.

Clay takes special care of his animals. He feeds them and gives them water every day.

Eva Geronimo

I'm Clay's mother, Eva Geronimo. We are proud that Geronimo is our **ancestor**. I am also proud of my son, Clay. Clay loves to play his guitar and his drum, and he loves to sing Western music.

I work with the Apache Elderly Program. We take elderly, or older, people into the mountains to gather **traditional** Indian **medicines** and wild foods. Clay often comes with me. He is learning to speak Apache from the older people.

Eva Geronimo has made teaching the traditional ways of the Apache a part of her life.

Robert Geronimo

I am Eva's brother, Robert Geronimo. My wife and I live near Eva and Clay with our children and grandchildren. I helped to build many of the roads that run through the reservation.

We are very proud to be Apache. The Apache Nation is made up of nine bands, or groups. Each band includes **clans** and other related families. Many Apache bands settled here in the Southwest in the early 1900s.

Robert was a rodeo cowboy when he was young. A rodeo is a contest in which cowboys and cowgirls show off their riding skills.

11

Apache Ways:
Alive and Strong

I'm Ellyn Bigrope. My family and grandchildren live near Clay's family on the reservation. I enjoy talking with school groups and visitors about Apache history. They ask me many questions about the Apache way of life.

Ellyn believes that it's important to teach others about Apache history.

We have many **celebrations**. Our biggest celebration is the Coming of Age Ceremony. It lasts for four days in July. During this time, Apache girls prepare to become women. Every piece of clothing in the celebration has meaning. We believe that different objects bring special powers to the wearer.

The Coming of Age Ceremony is a big part of a young Apache woman's life.

Apache Dances

Native American dances and rodeo events during the Coming of Age Ceremony bring people together. The families prepare big feasts and work hard to make sure everyone has something to eat.

Each of the four days has a Dance of the Apache **Maidens** and a Dance of the Mountain Gods. Dancers wear traditional and colorful clothes. Some say these clothes bring success to people.

 Dancing is an important part of the Apache Coming of Age Ceremony.

Dance of the Mountain Gods

The Dance of the Mountain Gods celebrates living and healing. The dance started long ago. A very old story tells how two boys were saved from evil spirits by the mountain gods. These gods showed the boys a special dance. Today, Apaches do the Dance of the Mountain Gods to drive away sickness and problems from their lives. Apaches believe the dance brings good health and happiness to those who see it.

The Dance of the Mountain Gods is performed around a fire at night. It reminds the Apache people of the dance's beginnings.

An Apache Medicine Woman

My name is Meredith Begay. I am an Apache medicine woman. My husband is Navajo. His grandfather was a medicine man. Our family is full of leaders and healers!

My work with the plants and medicines of the Apache people gives me peace. It is a big part of my life and who I am. It helps to keep us all strong.

Meredith is an Apache medicine woman, and is respected by the Apache people.

Prayers and Food

Medicine women often guide the Apache maidens through their duties for the Coming of Age Ceremony. Each day of the celebration, a special prayer is said before dawn. It is important to the Apache that everyone is blessed.

Fried bread is made at Apache celebrations. Corn soup, potato salad, and chili are other favorite foods. On the last day, people cook traditional foods, like wild spinach and wild beans.

The Apache gather under traditional teepees during the Coming of Age Ceremony. Apache foods are served at celebrations.

The Future of the Apache

I am Crystal Geronimo. My friends and I think we are lucky to live here in the mountains of southern New Mexico. More than 3,000 Apache people live here.

Apache kids like my brother Clay and me have a colorful history. Thanks to strong leaders and traditions, we have exciting futures ahead of us.

Glossary

ancestor   A relative who lived before you.

celebration   A special event during which the importance of something is honored.

clan   People who are related within a tribe.

maiden   A girl or young woman who has not yet married.

medicine   Something used to prevent or cure sickness.

medicine man or woman   A Native American who is believed to have power to heal the sick.

related   Belonging to the same family.

reservation   Land set aside by the government for Native Americans to live on.

sacred   Something that is highly respected and thought of as very important.

traditional   The way a group of people has done something for a long time.

Index